# Kate Middleton

## A Biography of the Duchess of Cambridge

BENJAMIN SOUTHERLAND

Copyright © 2017 Benjamin Southerland
All rights reserved. Neither this book nor any portion thereof may be reproduced or used in any manner whatsoever without the express written permission. Published in the United States of America.

Cover photo by Carfax2 is licensed under CC BY-SA 3.0 / Modified from original.

Visit Benjamin Southerland's website at benjaminsoutherland.com.

ISBN-13: 978-1520927732

# Table of Contents

Chapter 1: Kate—An Introduction ................................. 1
Chapter 2: Kate's Childhood ........................................ 4
    Kate's Parents ............................................................ 4
    Kate's Younger Years ................................................. 6
Chapter 3: University Life and the Courtship ............... 12
Chapter 4: The Wedding ............................................. 21
    Kate's Preparation ..................................................... 22
    The Wedding Dress .................................................. 22
    The Ceremony ......................................................... 24
    The Celebrations ...................................................... 26
    Pippa Middleton ....................................................... 30
Chapter 5: Reaction to Kate ........................................ 31
    Camilla Parker-Bowles ............................................. 32
    Prince Harry ............................................................. 34
    The Kate Middleton Effect ........................................ 36
Chapter 6: Life as a Royal .......................................... 39
    Children ................................................................... 39
    Official Duties .......................................................... 42
    Official Tours ........................................................... 44
    Activities While on Official Duties and Tours .......... 47
    Charity Work ........................................................... 49
    Honors and Awards .................................................. 50
    Coat of Arms ........................................................... 50
    Relationship with William ........................................ 51
About the Author ....................................................... 55

# Chapter 1: Kate—An Introduction

Kate Middleton's story seems like a modern-day fairytale; a girl from relatively humble beginnings is now a beautiful young woman living the life of a princess.

Catherine, Duchess of Cambridge; her husband, Prince William; and brother-in-law, Prince Harry, have endeared themselves to people worldwide with their down-to-earth nature, easy-going and cheerful demeanor and accessibility.

As interest in the royals continues to grow and they gain legions of new fans, interest grows in their pasts. For Kate, such questions arise: What has made Kate the woman she is today? How did Kate meet her prince? What is her life like now?

Kate grew up in an upper-middle-class family, spending most of her childhood in England with her parents and younger siblings (a brother and sister). She was extremely sporty and performed well academically. After a gap year, Kate attended the University of St Andrew's to earn an art history degree. It was there that she forged a relationship with Prince William, who had commenced study at the university the same year. They both resided in St Salvator's Hall their first year, and then rented out a townhouse with two other friends for the remainder of their university education.

Kate and William continued their relationship following graduation; however, reportedly owing to the lack of time they could spend together as a result of William's military training, they decided to take a break in April 2007. They reunited, and were engaged in October 2010. The Duke and Duchess of Cambridge were married on April 29, 2011, in a wedding watched by an estimated 300 million people worldwide.

Catherine, as she is now officially referred to, and William have two children, Prince George (born July 22, 2013) and Princess Charlotte (born May 2, 2015). Catherine suffered severe morning sickness during both pregnancies, resulting in short hospitalizations and a reduction in her official duties for the terms of her pregnancies.

Catherine continues to be a style icon, with items of clothing she is photographed wearing regularly selling out within hours of images being published. She also continues to demonstrate a refreshing sense of normalcy, mixing clothing from chain stores, luxury brands and little-known designers in her outfits, in addition to re-wearing items of clothes from time to time. Catherine also takes special care to support British designers in addition to the designers of countries she has officially toured.

# Chapter 2: Kate's Childhood

Catherine Elizabeth Middleton was born on January 9, 1982, at Royal Berkshire Hospital in Reading, England, and christened at St Andrew's Church in Bradfield, Berkshire, on June 20, 1982.

She is the eldest child of Michael Middleton and Carole Middleton (née Goldsmith), and has a younger sister, Philippa, and younger brother, James.

## Kate's Parents

Kate's father, Michael Francis Middleton, was born in 1949 in Leeds. His father was a pilot called Captain Peter Middleton, who flew with Prince Philip in 1962 as his co-pilot during a tour to South America. His grandfather was a lawyer who married an aristocrat (her family was described as "woolen manufacturers and landed gentry; a political and business dynasty"). Many of Michael Middleton's relatives were solicitors in the Leeds-based family firm, Middleton and Sons.

Michael was educated at a public school that is an older established school, often selective in the students it will enroll, and is an expensive fee-paying independent secondary school. The description "public" merely denotes that any member of the paying public may apply to attend, as opposed to schools that are limited to local residents or schools limited to members of a particular church.

He attended Clifton College in Bristol and boarded at Brown's House. He was a college prefect and represented Clifton College at rugby in the 1st XV and gained his tennis colors. Instead of studying at Oxford University, which was an expected family tradition, Michael became a British Airways (BA) flight attendant before graduating from their internal training to become a flight dispatcher.

Kate's mother, Carole Elizabeth Middleton (née Goldsmith) was born at Perivale Maternity Hospital to Dorothy Harrison and Ronald Goldsmith. She was raised in Southall in public housing and attended the local state schools. Carole's ancestors are described as working-class laborers and miners from Sunderland and County Durham.

Carole worked at British Airways as a flight attendant, and this is where she met her husband, Michael. They were married on June 21, 1980, in the Church of St James in Dorney, Buckinghamshire.

Carole's younger brother is IT recruitment multi-millionaire Gary Goldsmith.

In the 1980s, Kate's parents established Party Pieces, a mail-order business. Although it started out by making party bags, it extended to selling party supplies and decorations. By 1995 it was so successful that it was forced to move premises so it could accommodate all its business activities.

In addition to the couple launching their successful business, Michael inherited significant trust funds from his grandmother. As such, the Middletons have been described as an upper-middle-class family, and self-made millionaires.

## Kate's Younger Years

Kate and her family lived in Amman, Jordan, from May 1984 to September 1986 where her father Michael worked as a manager for British Airways. Upon their return, they lived in Chapel Row, a village near Newbury, Berkshire, England.

Kate's education followed that of her father in her attendance at selective, exclusive independent schools. At four years old, Kate was enrolled in the co-educational independent primary school St Andrew's School near her home, where she was educated until she was 13 years old (from 1986 to 1995). She boarded there for part of the week during her final two years. It is said that she saw Prince William for the first time in 1991, when he attended St Andrew's School for a match as part of the Ludgrove School hockey team when he was nine years old. However, royal sources have stated that Kate has no recollection of seeing Prince William then.

Kate revealed, during a visit to St Andrew's School in November 2012, that she and her sister Philippa were given the nicknames Pippa and Squeak, and that they gave their guinea pigs the same names. At a speech during that visit, she recalled that she loved her time at the school so much that when it was time for her to leave, she told her mother that she intended to return as a teacher. She also spoke of discovering her love of sport at the school. Kate's 1.50 m high-jump record, set in 1995, had still not been beaten at the time she returned for her visit as the Duchess of Cambridge. Kate's other sporting records included being the leading goal scorer for her hockey team, which she also captained, and she also still held the joint record for the 4 x 100 m relay at the time of her visit. Kate's deputy head, Paul Outram, recalled Kate to be a "cheerful and affable" pupil.

In addition to being active in sports, Kate also sang in the choir and played first the recorder and then the flute in the school orchestra. She also participated in school dramas, performing the role of Prince Charming in *Cinderella* and Eliza Doolittle in *My Fair Lady*.

Kate remembers a "wonderful and secure childhood," illustrated by stories such as having sister "camping parties" in the backyard of their family's first home, called West View, in Royal Berkshire when Kate and Pippa were young. Their home has been described as a fairy-tale-looking Victorian brick cottage that was purchased by Kate's parents in 1979 and sold by the family in 1995.

After completing her education at St Andrew's School, in 1996, Kate attended the all-girls' Downe House School in Berkshire for only two terms. There has been no official statement on her short stay at the school, although reports have speculated that she was bullied. The now-retired headmistress at the time, Susan Cameron, was interviewed by *The Mail on Sunday* (a UK newspaper) and despite insisting she was not aware of instances of bullying, acknowledged that Kate was "unsettled and not particularly happy." Susan suggested a number of reasons for this, such as the absence of field hockey from the curriculum (which Kate had already developed a passion for) and the difficulties associated with changing to a school that had a vastly different environment, which Downe House was in comparison to St Andrew's School. However, Susan did note that all-girl environments could be cliquey and "rather cruel." Susan recalled meeting with Kate's parents, who informed her they had received a recommendation from the head teacher at Kate's previous school that she move to Marlborough College, which she accepted.

While it was very unusual to switch schools during an academic year, Kate became a boarder at the co-educational, elite Marlborough College, located in Wiltshire, in term three. It was a school filled with aristocrats and royalty, where girls wore floor-length black skirts reminiscent of the Victorian era and flamboyant parties were held in stately homes (although they were more relaxed than the formality of the school). One of the students there, Jessica Hay, described Kate as "pale, quiet, shy, a little bullied" and said that she heard Kate crying herself to sleep.

Nevertheless, in an article in *The Guardian*, Clarissa Sebag-Montefiore described Kate as "ordinary, hard-working, athletic and easy-going," and it appears she settled in well; she was an eager participant in many sports and excelled in many of them, including tennis, field hockey, swimming, netball and rounders (an old English game that shares similarities with softball and baseball).

Kate's classmates have described her as level-headed, popular and talented. Charlie Leslie stated, "Kate is an absolutely phenomenal girl—really popular, talented, creative and sporty. She was captain of the school hockey team and played in the first pair at tennis," although it was noted that she was not "the brightest button." A college master at Marlborough College said, "I don't think you'd find anyone in Marlborough with a bad word to say about her. She excelled in all her subjects and was an A-grade pupil across the board."

Like many teenage girls, Kate was not immune to developing crushes. It is reported that while at Marlborough College, 14-year-old Kate developed a crush on a tennis sports star at the school called Woody Webster, with whom she shared her first kiss. Kate's favorite film for a time was the movie *Cocktail* and it followed that her celebrity crush was Tom Cruise.

Kate dated during her high school years, including the person said to be her first serious boyfriend, Harry Blakelock, who was a year older than she was. The relationship ended when he graduated a year before her and left for a gap year. Kate also dated Willem Marx during high school. Kate was single during her own gap year, part of which was spent in Florence.

Although it is often thought that Kate and William first met at St Andrews, it appears they met a few years before, in the summer of 1999, when Kate was around 17 years old. She spent time with Prince William's and Prince Harry's inner circle known as the Glossy Posse when she was invited to a few of the Glossy Posse's parties through mutual friends. She told a friend in Florence that she'd met the prince "once or twice."

# Chapter 3: University Life and the Courtship

Kate initially planned to attend the University of Edinburgh and applied for art history, for which she received a letter of acceptance. A number of her friends were also planning to attend the established and well-regarded university in Scotland. However, Kate made a sudden decision to drop her place and take a gap year, before re-applying to study the history of art at the University of St Andrew's. St Andrew's was already the most difficult university in Scotland to gain admission to, and applications to St Andrew's increased by almost 50 percent when the palace announced that Prince William was going there.

Both Kate and William started their studies at the university in 2001, and were art history students residing in rooms close to each other at St Salvator's Hall, when their friendship began. It has even been reported that Kate convinced William to stay at university when he was finding it difficult to settle. He eventually switched to studying geography. During this time, it appears that they built a strong foundation for a relationship through their developing friendship, with Kate dating another pupil at the university called Rupert Finch.

Kate began sharing a four-bedroom townhouse with William and two other friends at the start of their second academic year in September 2002, before the four moved into a cottage outside the town for their third year. All four were often seen out on the town, drinking in bars such as Ma Bells or dining at eateries such as the Jahangir Indian restaurant.

It is reported that Kate's turn as a model in a 2002 St Andrew's Fashion Show, wearing Charlotte Todd's humble dress, a £30 see-through number made of black and gold silk knitted together with a blue ribbon trim, was the moment that she caught William's eye as more than friendship material.

Kate and William continued to spend time together as friends, which included watching rugby in May 2003 and Kate's attendance at William's 21st birthday party at Windsor Castle in 2003. Unofficial reports indicate Kate may have started dating William around the Christmas in 2003 following her split from her previous boyfriend. Kate and William were first seen in public on a ski trip in

Klosters in April 2004, and officials did not deny they were dating.

William and Kate spent weekends together in a secluded cottage at the queen's Balmoral estate while continuing their studies, and despite media speculation of an engagement in 2005, Kate did not attend the wedding of William's father, the Prince of Wales, to Camilla Parker Bowles. However, Kate did accompany William to the wedding of his close friend Hugh van Cutsem shortly after.

In November 2005, Kate graduated from the University of St Andrew's with a master of arts (a four-year undergraduate honors degree), with upper second-class honors. Kate and William graduated at the same ceremony and were joined by their families to share a lunch together in celebration.

In October 2005 and again in January 2007, Kate Middleton's lawyers (the same as those used by the Prince of Wales), issued complaints about media harassment. Then in December 2005, the German magazine *Das Nee* published photos of the exterior of Kate's London flat (purchased by her parents for their children), and in doing so, revealed its location. This resulted in a security review by police following concerns for her safety. It was also reported in the *London Evening Standard* that Prince William was considering going to the European Court of Human Rights regarding his and Kate's privacy. Given the circumstances surrounding the death of his mother, Diana, Princess of Wales, his cautious response is unsurprising.

In February 2006, it was announced that Kate would receive her own 24-hour security detail, supplied by the Royalty and Diplomatic Protection Department, which only fuelled speculation of an upcoming engagement; she would not be entitled to this service, otherwise. However, an engagement did not follow and Kate was not provided with an allowance to fund the security detail.

During this time, Kate and William continued to date and were photographed kissing in public for the first time, during a skiing holiday in Klosters, Switzerland, in January 2006. William commenced training at the Royal Military Academy Sandhurst upon their return from Switzerland, although Kate remained connected with the Royal family, with an invitation to the Royal Box at the Cheltenham Gold Cup in March. William's father and stepmother were also present.

In April, Kate and William took an opportunity to spend time together during a break in William's training, at Mustique, a Caribbean island. The next month, they attended the wedding of William's stepsister Laura

Parker Bowles. They again holidayed together, this time in Ibiza, during another break in William's training.

In November 2006, Kate started working part-time as an accessories buyer with the clothing chain Jigsaw (owned by family friends), before joining her family business, Party Pieces, in November 2007. Kate worked at Party Pieces until January 2011, which included responsibility for catalogue design and production, marketing and photography.

On December 15, 2006, Kate's position as a serious girlfriend was solidified when she attended William's Passing Out Parade at the Royal Military Academy Sandhurst as an official royal guest.

However, they did not spend Christmas together owing to the strict royal tradition of only royalty attending Christmas Day at Sandringham. William had agreed to spend New Year with the Middleton family at Jordanstone House, a large country house located in Scotland; however, he changed his mind, which upset Kate. The day before Kate's 25th birthday in March 2007, William joined his first regiment at Bovington Barracks in Dorset, which was a three-hour drive from London. Instead of returning to London regularly, William chose to spend time with his fellow soldiers in Dorset, and sometimes prioritized his friends over Kate when he did return to London.

The time spent apart, coupled with the unrelenting intense media scrutiny Kate had had to endure for over a year, appears to have taken a toll on the young adults; in April 2007, William and Kate decided to take a break. There was never any official reason for the split although it is speculated that, despite how clearly they loved each other, and how well they "fitted" together (as their friends described it), William had some doubts.

It appears that Kate had asked William to confirm his commitment to her, after her confidence in their relationship had been shaken by images that appeared in the media on a few occasions of him at nightclubs and flirting with other women. William was unwilling to make a long-term commitment, and the relationship ended.

William famously celebrated the end of his relationship by going to the Mahiki nightclub in London's West End with his friends, where he jumped on a table and shouted, "I'm free!" While Kate was devastated by the break-up, she also spent her new single status partying and having fun with her friends, which was unusual for the usually reserved and conservative girl. Kate's sister, Pippa, who had by then graduated from university, joined her in the Chelsea flat owned by their parents. In April and May, Kate and Pippa were photographed in risqué outfits at various exclusive events around London.

Kate and her family still attended the Concert for Diana at Wembley Stadium on July 1, 2007, although she sat two rows away from Prince William. They were seen together in public from time to time after that. Although there was never any official announcement that they had reunited, it is commonly thought their separation was not more than three months, and they may secretly have rekindled their relationship as early as June 9, 2007, when Kate attended a party at William's barracks to celebrate the end of his training.

During her engagement interview, she said of the breakup, "I think at the time I wasn't very happy about it, but actually it made me a stronger person, you find out things about yourself that maybe you hadn't realized. I think you can get quite consumed by a relationship when you're younger…I really valued that time for me as well, although I didn't think it at the time!"

Kate continued to maintain a strong a relationship with William's family despite his on-going absence due to his army commitments, attending Peter Phillips' (Prince William's cousin's) wedding to Autumn Kelly on May 17, 2008, unaccompanied by William. On July 19, 2008, she was a guest at the wedding of Lady Rose Windsor to George Gilman, again in William's absence (he was on military operations in the Caribbean).

Kate still endured the intrusion of the press, and an invasion of privacy complaint against two news agencies and a photographer, who took pictures of her at Christmas in 2009, was resolved in her favor, for which she received a public apology, £5,000 in damages and legal costs.

Despite the media attention she attracted, her relationship and its associated commitments, and her job within the family business, Kate found time to start performing unpublicized charity work, including secret visits to the Naomi House Children's Hospice, close to the Middletons' Bucklebury home.

William and Kate were engaged in October 2010 during a ten-day trip to the Lewa Wildlife Conservancy in Kenya to celebrate Prince William passing his RAF helicopter search and rescue course. Clarence House announced the engagement on November 16, 2010.

Kate and William gave an exclusive interview to ITV News' political editor Tom Bradby and a photocall was held at St James's Palace. The official engagement photographs were taken on November 25, 2010, by Mario Testino, and were released publicly the next month.

Of their engagement, Prince William said, "The timing is right now, we are both very, very happy." Kate noted that joining the royal family was a "daunting prospect" but said that "[h]opefully I'll take it in my stride."

Prince William gave Kate his late mother's sapphire and diamond engagement ring, which Diana, Princess of Wales, had been presented by Prince Charles. The wedding ring included an 18-karat white gold ring with a 12-carat oval Ceylon sapphire and 14 round diamonds. While it was originally a size H, Kate arranged for it to be resized to a size I.

# Chapter 4: The Wedding

Kate and William were married at Westminster Abbey in London on April 29, 2011 (St. Catherine's Day).

On the morning of the wedding, in accordance with royal tradition and as an acknowledgement to the important day, Queen Elizabeth conferred on William the titles of Duke of Cambridge, Earl of Strathearn and Baron of Carrickfergus. As a result, Kate, upon her marriage, was given the title of Catherine, Her Royal Highness the Duchess of Cambridge (referred to as Her Royal Highness Catherine, the Duchess of Cambridge), in addition to Countess of Strathearn in Scotland and Baroness of Carrickfergus in Ireland.

The wedding day was declared a bank holiday in the United Kingdom, and 26 million people watched the event live in Britain, with an estimated global audience of over 300 million.

## Kate's Preparation

Kate, her sister, Pippa, and mother, Carole, all stayed at the Goring Hotel in Belgravia the night before her wedding.

On the eve of her wedding, Kate visited the Jo Hansford Salon for a manicure. Following a hand exfoliation and deep-tissue massage, her manicurist, Marina Sandoval, took note of Kate's wish for a nail color that was off-white and bridal, and blended a few shades of polish, including Bourjois' Rose Lounge and Essie's Allure to create a custom shade suited to Kate's skin tone.

Kate also underwent two hours of hair preparation the evening before her wedding, including a wash, blow dry and curl, performed by hairdressers James Pryce and Richard Ward. In one of the suites reserved for the bridal party, the hairdressers started preparing Kate's hair in the demi-chignon she had chosen, at 6:30 a.m. on the day of the wedding, following months of planning.

## The Wedding Dress

In the lead up to the wedding, speculation as to which designer would design the wedding dress increased. On March 6, 2011, *The Sunday Times* quoted a fashion source as describing the dress as a collaboration between Kate and Sarah Burton, the creative director of luxury fashion house Alexander McQueen. Despite both Sarah and the fashion house denying involvement, Burton became the odds-on favorite amongst bookmakers.

Details of the dress and its maker were not formally announced until the bride stepped from her car to enter Westminster Abbey just prior to the service, and Sarah Burton was confirmed as the designer. Some controversy reigned regarding the choice of Sarah Burton, because the Italian company Gucci owned the fashion house Alexander McQueen, meaning that it was the first time a British-owned fashion house wasn't chosen for a British royal wedding.

It was reported that Kate first saw Sarah Burton's work at the wedding of Tom Parker Bowles, the son of Camilla, Duchess of Cornwall, when Sarah designed the bride Sara Buys' bridal gown.

The wedding dress itself was an ivory gown with lace applique floral detail and an intricate train, measure 2.7 m. Kate's dress went on display at Buckingham Palace from July 23, 2011, until October 3, 2011, during the annual summer exhibition.

Official records noted that Kate wished to combine tradition and modernity into the dress, and that she was heavily involved in its design.

The ivory satin bodice was padded slightly at the hips and narrowed at the waist, and was inspired by the

Victorian tradition of corsetry popular with Alexander McQueen. The bodice contained lace floral motifs, which were then appliquéd on to silk net (tulle) by the Royal School of Needlework in Hampton Court Palace. Fifty-eight buttons of gazar and organza featured on the rear of the dress. The skirt, underskirt trim and bridal train also incorporated appliquéd lace.

The main body of the dress was made in ivory and white satin gazar, using specially-sourced UK fabrics, with a long, full skirt reminiscent of an opening flower, with soft pleats that unfolded to the floor, forming a Victorian-style semi-bustle at the back. A blue ribbon was sewn inside the dress, to fulfill the "something blue" tradition, and the design for the bodice of the dress featuring lace in the style of the 19th Century was the "something old."

Kate's tiara was a 1936 Cartier Scroll tiara, which was loaned to her by the queen, a tradition for British royal weddings. To ensure the tiara did not fall off, the top of Kate's hair was backcombed forming a base for the tiara to sit on, with the tiara then sewn in.

## The Ceremony

The wedding was attended by Kate's and William's family, in addition to their personal guests, foreign royals, members of the British royal households, military officials, members of religious organizations and diplomats, totaling 1,900 guests. Given that, at the time, William was second in line to the throne rather than the heir apparent, the wedding was not a full state occasion, giving the couple greater freedom in deciding the details of the wedding. Kate chose to have the church decorated to resemble an English country garden, using 15-year-old maples to create a "living avenue" under which guests walked to their seats. The remainder of the church was decorated with cream and white flowers.

Kate arrived at Westminster Abbey by car (a Rolls-Royce Phantom VI) rather than a carriage, which traditionally transported royal brides to their wedding. Kate arrived at 11:00 a.m. and stepped on to the red carpet outside Westminster Abbey's Great West Door. It took Kate three and half minutes to walk up the aisle with her father to the coronation anthem "I Was Glad" by Sir Charles Hubert Hastings Parry.

Given the close relationship between the siblings on both sides, it is unsurprising that Kate's sister, Pippa, was the maid of honor, and Prince Harry was William's best man. Kate's brother, James, gave the lesson as part of the service. Kate was attended by four bridesmaids and two pageboys, all aged ten years and under.

Kate and William chose vows that did not require Kate to promise "to obey" her husband, which William's mother, Diana, Princess of Wales, also chose to omit from her vows. Instead, Kate vowed to "love, comfort, honor and keep" William.

William's father, Prince Charles, and his wife, the Duchess of Cornwall, along with Kate's parents and sister acted as witnesses and signed the marriage registers.

Kate and William left their wedding to the orchestral march "Crown Imperial" by William Walton, which was also played at William's parents' wedding.

In keeping with a tradition started by the late Queen Mother (Queen Elizabeth's mother), Kate placed her bouquet on the grave of the Unknown Warrior at Westminster Abbey after the ceremony.

## The Celebrations

Following the wedding, the couple returned to Buckingham Palace by carriage along a route that passed Parliament Square, Whitehall, Horse Guards Parade, Clarence House, and The Mall. The couple followed the royal tradition of appearing on the balcony of Buckingham Palace to watch the flypast of a variety of past and present military aircraft. Shortly after they appeared on the balcony, they were joined by the bridal party, and finally, by their families.

Approximately 600 people were invited to a luncheon reception at Buckingham Palace hosted by the queen, who saw the couple cut their eight-tiered wedding cake before she left Buckingham Palace for a weekend away. The fruitcake was covered in cream and white icing and decorated with 900 delicate sugar-paste flowers that took five weeks for a team of cake-makers to create. Kate did not want the cake to be towering and thin, so the first three layers were made of multiple cakes nestled under the remaining layers, which widened the base. Some of the architectural details in the Picture Hall, which served as the reception area, were incorporated into the decorations, in addition to 17 different foliage or flowers chosen by Kate for their meaning or symbolism: Rose - white (national symbol of England), Daffodil (national symbol of Wales, new beginnings), Shamrock (national symbol of Ireland), Thistle (national symbol of Scotland), Acorns and oak leaves (strength, endurance), Myrtle (love), Ivy (wedded love, marriage), Lily of the Valley (sweetness, humility), Rose - bridal (happiness, love), Sweet William (grant me one smile), Honeysuckle (the bond of love), Apple Blossom (preference, good fortune), White Heather (protection, wishes will come true), Jasmine - white (amiability), Daisy (innocence, beauty, simplicity), Orange Blossom (marriage, eternal love, fruitfulness) and Lavender (ardent attachment, devotion, success, and luck).

Prince William chose a chocolate biscuit cake for the groom's cake, which William and Harry used to eat when they were young. The biscuit manufacturer McVities made the cake from 1,700 biscuits and 17 kg of chocolate.

By the evening celebration, only 300 of Kate's and William's closest friends and family were invited to a black-tie dinner hosted by the Prince of Wales. It was described by a guest as "the most magical party imaginable," with Kate changing into another white gown by Sarah Burton, to enjoy the celebrations.

Guests travelled through a candle-lit walkway into the palace courtyard to the pre-dinner drinks reception, where they were welcomed by bagpipes. They were served vintage pink champagne, peach bellinis and elderflower cocktails.

At 8:00 p.m., the guests entered the ballroom, which was decorated with white flowers and candles. All of the tables had been named after places that were of special significance to their friends and family. Given that their friends and family were considered "equally important" to the couple, there was a mix of royals, family members and friends at each table. The food was locally sourced, including seafood from Wales and lamb from Highgrove.

After the speeches, the guests were ushered into the throne room, which had been turned into a nightclub, where they were treated to cocktails, spirits, and mojito cocktails, and could rest on sofas when not on the dance floor. Pop star Ellie Goulding provided a two-hour performance before DJs took over. At 2:00 a.m., waiters served bacon sandwiches to the guests, before they congregated on the palace gardens for a 3:00 a.m. fireworks display. A Catherine wheel exploded as Kate and William were driven away in a convertible vintage Fiat 500, standing in the car with their heads through the open-topped roof, although they simply drove around the corner; they spent their first night together as husband and wife at Buckingham Palace.

Kate and William asked that donations be made to charities instead of receiving traditional wedding gifts. They established The Prince William and Miss Catherine Middleton Charitable Gift Fund and selected a number of charities across the Commonwealth that would benefit from the fund.

Kate and William honeymooned for ten days in the Seychelles, in a £4,000-a-night bungalow on North Island. Their villa had its own butler, a private garden and freshwater rock pool. They also enjoyed a sunset cruise and champagne picnic while there.

Upon their return, William and Kate resided on the Isle of Anglesey in North Wales, where William was based as a RAF Search and Rescue pilot, following his transfer from the British Army to the Royal Air Force.

## Pippa Middleton

On the day of the royal wedding, one of the most immediate reactions was to Kate's matron of honor; her sister Pippa wore a white figure-hugging dress, which, like the bride's, was created by Sarah Burton. It was made of ivory crêpe fabric, with a cowl at the front and organza-covered buttons at the back.

However, it was the figure-hugging nature that caught the public's attention; as she carried Kate's train, Pippa's backside almost immediately gained a Facebook page, called the Pippa Middleton Ass Appreciation Society. The Pippa Buttlift became a known plastic surgery option and was the inspiration for some bottom-boosting underwear.

# Chapter 5: Reaction to Kate

Despite a positive reaction to Kate from the public, Kate and her family endured a difficult period, during which the class-obsessed British noted their humble origins; they were from a commoner background (meaning they had no connection to nobility or royalty) rather than the aristocracy, which was considered more suitable for royalty.

The journey to acceptance was not easy. It was rumored that William's aristocratic friends used to whisper "door to manual" when Kate entered the room, which is an instruction given by the pilot to the crew after landing, and was intended as a derogatory comment on her mother's former job as a flight attendant.

Carole chewed gum at William's graduation ceremony at Sandhurst, and the media declared it evidence that Kate was not "posh" enough to marry a prince. Further, it was rumored that Carole had asked for "the toilet" at a royal function, instead of using the upper-class terminology "the loo" or "lavatory."

At the time of the troubled relationship between William and Kate, reports indicated that Kate was very aware of the snobbery she and her family faced, with her primary concern being for the wellbeing of her family.

In fact, Kate is the first working-class woman ("non-blueblood") to marry into the royal family in modern history; the last time it happened was in 1660. Therefore, Kate has become an example of the upward mobility possible in modern England, in addition to demonstrating that the royal family is prepared to relax tradition and become more relevant in today's society.

Whether acceptance of Kate into the royal family was reluctant, or a relatively easy decision after seeing how happy William was, has been the subject of much speculation, with reports that the Duchess of Cornwall, in particular, thought Kate was "too common" and encouraged Prince Charles to urge his son to reconsider his relationship with Kate. This was despite the fact that Kate was set to become the first royal bride to hold a degree.

## Camilla Parker-Bowles

Of course, there has never been any official comment regarding Camilla's opinion of Kate; however, despite an apparently pleasant initial meeting while Kate was still a student at the University of St Andrew's, persistent rumors have abounded over the years that Camilla never intended that Kate should become a member of the royal family.

In fact, Camilla apparently saw Kate as pretty but "rather dim," and did not consider a commoner to be suitable wife material for William. Instead, Camilla had hoped that William would marry an aristocrat, and ideally a member of one of the royal houses of Europe.

Camilla is also said to have disliked Kate's mother, Carole, due to her smoking habit and "gauche and pushy" demeanor.

It is speculated that one of the reasons why Camilla was so against the relationship was because, at the time, public opinion of her was low, and she was jealous of the attention given to a beautiful young woman, instead of her. This is alleged to be the reason why Kate did not attend the wedding of Prince Charles to Camilla; Kate was not invited so she could not upstage the bride.

Camilla maintained a strong influence over Prince Charles, and used her influence to sway Prince Charles' counsel to William when he was having doubts about his relationship with Kate. Camilla is therefore credited with contributing to the temporary break in their relationship in 2007. However, once William decided that he wanted to make a commitment to Kate, Prince Charles was unswerving in his support for his son.

Despite those reports, there are many recent images of Kate and Camilla in the press, looking at each other as they share a laugh, and it is not difficult to see genuine affection in their eyes. Whether this represents a thawing in Camilla's opinion of Kate, or that they have always shared a close relationship, is certainly never going to be discussed officially.

## Prince Harry

From the very start of Kate's relationship with William, Harry has been welcoming. Both William and Harry knew that their mother did not have an easy entry into the royal family following her marriage to Prince Charles, and they have actively supported Kate as she has learned to adjust to life in the spotlight and then as a royal.

In fact, when Harry learned of his brother's intention to propose to Kate, he gave William their mother's engagement ring; after her death, both boys had been permitted to select some of Princess Diana's personal items as keepsakes. While Harry chose her engagement ring, William chose a £19,000 watch. However, they swapped so that Kate could be presented with Diana's ring.

Following the engagement, Kate and Harry were often pictured together, usually caught in the middle of a fit of laughter. As Kate appeared at more and more functions, Harry seemed to be nearby providing her with support, especially if William was busy with royal duties.

Following the wedding in 2011, Harry said, "To have a big sister is very, very nice. I've got to know Catherine pretty well, but now that she's becoming a part of the family, I'm really looking forward to getting her under my wing, or she'll be taking me under her wing probably."

Since the wedding, though William and Kate could have focused on their life together and Harry could have continued his busy life himself, William, Kate and Harry have formed an even stronger bond, often attending functions together, in addition to sharing a charitable trust and a royal household together.

The public's response to Kate has been almost the complete opposite of the general reaction by the aristocracy. The media has acknowledged this; for example, she was named in *The Daily Telegraph* as the "Most Promising Newcomer" in its 2006 list of winners and losers, and in 2012 and 2013, she was included on *Time* magazine's list as one of the 100 Most Influential People in the World.

# The Kate Middleton Effect

Blessed with physical beauty and a healthy body as a result of her love of sports (and, no doubt, genetics), it is unsurprising that Kate has become very influential when it comes to fashion (particularly in Britain and America), known as the Kate Middleton Effect.

This has been reflected in the media: Kate was number one on *Vanity Fair* magazine's annual best-dressed list in 2010, 2011, 2012 and 2013; *Tatler* placed her at number 8 on its yearly listing of the top ten style icons in 2007; she featured in *People* magazine's 2007 and 2010 best-dressed lists in addition to *Vanity Fair* magazine's international best-dressed list in July 2008. In 2016, Kate appeared on the cover of *Vogue* magazine's centenary issue, which was her first magazine shoot.

However, Kate's influence in fashion has been best reflected in the remarkable public reaction to the outfits she wears. From the blue Issa dress she wore to announce her engagement in November 2010, which sold out in the US and UK within 24 hours of her appearance in it, to the floral print maxi dress by label Glamorous that she wore on tour in India in April 2016 while visiting a contact center run by the charity Salaam Baalak, which sold out in two hours, public approval of her fashion choices has not waned over the years.

Beyond the enormous popularity of the actual outfits she has worn, Kate seems to have sparked general trends, such as a season filled with blue dresses on red carpets, "little blue dresses," and coral-colored jeans.

Kate has also increased brand awareness. She wears a mix of chain-store clothing (such as Zara; for example, she wore a £20 faux crystal necklace with an expensive Roland Mouret gown at a red carpet film premiere), little known brands and luxury brands, in addition to re-wearing clothes. For example, Reiss noticed an increase in terms of brand interest and awareness globally after Kate wore a dress from the brand to meet the Obamas in 2011. The dress sold out online after access was restored following the website crashing owing to the web traffic following released images of Kate in the dress. Kate also wore a pink and teal dress by Indian designer Anita Dongre to play cricket in during her tour of India, and within hours the designer's website had crashed due to the volume of traffic. Kate's own style was added to the dress, with Kate and her people making a fabric belt with tassels out of a scarf that was a part of the original dress.

In addition to her influence in fashion, Kate has been credited with increasing public support for the royals; in the 1990s and early 2000s, support was at an all-time low, following a number of incidents that gave rise to the public impression that the royals were out of touch. The new breed of younger royals, including William, Harry and Kate, seems to have spearheaded an institution less steeped in tradition and more accessible to the public.

Wearing chain-store clothing and accessories has helped Kate appear more relatable, in addition to her comfort in re-wearing clothes, such as Russell and Bromley four-inch cork wedge shoes, which she has worn with jeans and has also played volleyball in; a quirky Anya Hindmarch handbag, which she took to Wimbledon in July 2014 and on her official tour to Canada; and Hobbs' white and grey Wessex dress, which has been worn a number of times over the course of three years.

Kate has also been known to purchase items on sale or wear items that are seasons old, such as the Whistles blouse she wore in her royal engagement photos.

# Chapter 6: Life as a Royal

## Children

On December 3, 2012, St James's Palace announced that Kate was pregnant with her first child. This was announced earlier than a traditional announcement, because of Kate's admission to King Edward VII's Hospital suffering from hyperemesis gravidarum, a severe form of morning sickness. She was treated for three days before being released. St James's Palace provided an update on January 14, 2013, assuring that Kate's health was improving and that the Duke and Duchess were expecting their child in July 2013.

However, the news was marred by controversy when, in December 2012, two Australian radio hosts, Michael Christian and Mel Greig from 2Day FM, called the hospital. Pretending to be the Queen and the Prince of Wales, they spoke to a nurse on Kate's ward, asking about her condition. Just days later, following a hospital inquiry and a public backlash against the hoax, the nurse who put the call through to the ward, Jacintha Saldanha, committed suicide, citing the radio hosts' actions as a contributing factor in deciding to take her own life. Kate and William released a statement that they were "deeply saddened" and that "their thoughts and prayers [were] with Jacintha Saldanha's family, friends and colleagues at this very sad time."

Kate was admitted to the Lindo Wing of St Mary's Hospital in London in the early stages of labor on the morning of July 22, 2013, and gave birth to a boy, weighing eight pounds and six ounces (3.80 kg) at 4:24 p.m. that day. As per tradition, the announcement of the birth was made by the placing of an easel in the forecourt of Buckingham Palace, detailing the birth.

Kate and William appeared with their new son on the steps of the hospital the next day, after Kate was discharged from the hospital. Kate was widely praised for her decision to display her bump, which is natural following birth, and is known as a "mummy tummy" (it usually takes around ten days for the womb to contract back to its normal size following birth). Kate wore a Jenny Packham pale blue polka-dot dress made especially for her discharge from hospital, which appeared to be a nod to the late Princess of Wales' green polka-dot dress worn as she left the hospital with William. Kate's hair stylist attended the hospital to help her prepare for this significant public appearance.

On July 24, 2013, Kensington Palace announced the baby had been named George Alexander Louis. His official title is His Royal Highness Prince George of Cambridge, and he is third in line to the throne.

The next month, the first official photograph of George was released by Kensington Palace, showing William, Kate, George and Lupo, the family's pet Cocker Spaniel, at the Middleton family home. Kate's father took the photo, as opposed to the traditional formal photos ordinarily taken and released.

Prince George's arrival prompted the breaking of further royal tradition, with Kate's parents invited to spend Christmas at Sandringham so he could spend his first Christmas with both sets of grandparents.

Kate's second pregnancy was announced on September 8, 2014. Kate again suffered hyperemesis gravidarum and missed a number of engagements. On May 2, 2015, at 8:34 a.m., Kate gave birth to a girl weighing eight pounds and three ounces (3.71 kg), the fourth in line to the throne.

Once again, Kate was discharged from the hospital quickly, appearing with her baby and William on the steps of the hospital less than ten hours after giving birth, and once again, wearing a custom-made Jenny Packham dress, this time in yellow. Her hairdresser once again attended the hospital to style her hair.

On May 4, 2015, Kensington Palace announced the baby had been named Charlotte Elizabeth Diana. Her official title is Her Royal Highness Princess Charlotte of Cambridge.

## Official Duties

Although not yet a royal, Kate was formally introduced to public life on February 24, 2011, (two months before the wedding) when she and Prince William attended a lifeboat-naming ceremony in Trearddur, Anglesey, in North Wales. On February 25, 2011, they appeared at the University of St Andrew's to launch its 600th anniversary celebrations.

Kate's first official engagement was in May 2011 when she and William met the president of the United States, Barack Obama, and the first lady, Michelle Obama.

In June and July 2011, Kate and William undertook their first official tour as a married couple to Canada and the United States.

On October 26, 2011, Kate undertook her first solo event for In Kind Direct, stepping in for the Prince of Wales, who was overseas.

On November 2, 2011, Kate and William visited the UNICEF Supply Division Centre in Copenhagen, Denmark, which supplied food to malnourished African children.

Kate's first solo military engagement was on March 17, 2012, when she carried out the traditional awarding of shamrocks to the Irish Guards at their base in Aldershot on St. Patrick's Day.

On March 19, 2012, Kate gave her first speaking engagement for the opening of the Treehouse, a new children's hospice opened by East Anglia's Children's Hospices (EACH), a charity of which she is a patron.

In June 2012, The Foundation of Prince William and Prince Harry was renamed The Royal Foundation of the Duke and Duchess of Cambridge and Prince Harry, to reflect Kate's contribution to the charity.

Kate and William were announced as ambassadors for the 2012 Summer Olympics in London, alongside Prince Harry, and as part of her role, Kate attended sporting events throughout the Games.

In September 2012, Kate and William toured Singapore, Malaysia, Tuvalu and the Solomon Islands as part of the Queen's Diamond Jubilee celebrations. During this tour, Kate made her first official speech abroad, while visiting a hospice in Malaysia.

In April 2014, Kate and William undertook their first official tour with their new son, to New Zealand and Australia. The tour was Kate's first visit to the area and George's first major public appearance since his christening in October 2013.

Kate was to undertake her first solo trip, to the island of Malta in September 2014, for its 50th independence anniversary celebrations. Her trip was cancelled, however, after the announcement of her second pregnancy in early September, with William taking her place.

## Official Tours

- June 30–July 8, 2011
    - Canada: Ontario, Quebec, Prince Edward Island, Northwest Territories, Alberta
- July 8–10, 2011
    - United States: Los Angeles
    - Notable: Attended a BAFTA event
- November 2, 2011
    - Denmark: Copenhagen
    - Notable: visit to the UNICEF Headquarters
- September 11–13, 2012

- Singapore
- Notable: Diamond Jubilee Tour on behalf of the queue

- September 13–15, 2012
  - Malaysia: Kuala Lumpur, Sabah
  - Notable: Diamond Jubilee Tour on behalf of the queen

- September 16–18, 2012
  - Solomon Islands: Honiara, Tavanipupu
  - Notable: Diamond Jubilee Tour on behalf of the queen

- September 18–19, 2012
  - Tuvalu: Funafuti
  - Notable: Diamond Jubilee Tour on behalf of the queen

- April 7–16, 2014
  - New Zealand: Wellington, Blenheim, Auckland, Hamilton, Cambridge, Dunedin, Queenstown, Christchurch
  - Notable: Accompanied by Prince George

- April 16–25, 2014
    - Australia: Sydney, Brisbane, Uluru, Adelaide, Canberra
    - Notable: Accompanied by Prince George
- June 6, 2014
    - France: Arromanches
    - Notable: Commemoration of the 70th anniversary of the Normandy landings at Gold Beach
- August 4, 2014
    - Belgium: Liege
    - Notable: World War I centenary commemorations at the Cointe Inter-allied Memorial, and the Saint Symphorien Military Cemetery
- April 10–13, 2016
    - India: Mumbai, Delhi, Kaziranga
- April 14–15, 2016
    - Bhutan: Thimphu
- April 16, 2016

- India: Agra

- Notable: Visited the Taj Mahal in Agra and sat on the same bench that William's late mother was photographed on

In addition to being a supporter of British fashion designers, Kate tends to acknowledge local fashion designers while on tour, or those that at least have a tie to the country, such as the printed Prabal Gurung dress she wore during her trip to Singapore in 2012, which was made by an American-Nepalese designer who was born in Singapore.

# Activities While on Official Duties and Tours

Kate is well known to be very active while performing official duties and touring overseas. For example, she

- donned a helmet, vest and windbreaker while sailing with the Land Rover BAR team during a visit to Ben Ainslie Racing in Portsmouth, England, in May 2016, as part of her duties as a patrol of Sir Ben Ainslie's sailing charity, the 1851 Trust;

- played field hockey in November 2012 at St Andrew's School in Berkshire—she played on the team while attending school there, and again played hockey in March 2012 at London's Olympic Park before meeting the Great Britain men's and women's teams;

- tried archery while visiting Bhutan;

- played cricket in India while in wedges, and again played cricket while in Australia;

- tried boxing with former boxer Duke McKenzie during the launch of Heads Together on May, 16, 2016;

- played soccer at a children's camp in India in wedged heels;

- went rock climbing in the rainforests of Borneo with William;

- beat William twice in sailing races, while touring in Australia in April 2013;

- played volleyball in October 2013, three months after giving birth to Prince George, at a SportsAid athletic workshop;

- had a game of table tennis against William during an April 2013 visit to the Donald Dewar Leisure Centre in Glasgow, Scotland, and also played a bit of basketball;

- participated in a ball-throwing exercise with students from Percy Hedley School during an October 2012 visit to Newcastle Civic Centre;

- and learned local dance moves while visiting Malaysia in September 2012.

Kate and William undertook an hours-long hike in Bhutan, reaching the top looking fit and not having broken a sweat. They followed in the footsteps of Prince Charles who had also taken the same walk but stopped halfway up to paint the beautiful scenery.

# Charity Work

In March 2011, Kate and William established a gift fund to allow well-wishers who wanted to give them a wedding gift to donate money to charities instead. The couple chose 26 charities to be supported by the fund, including charities benefiting the armed forces, children, the elderly, art, sport and conservation.

Kate is patron to:

- The Art Room
- National Portrait Gallery
- East Anglia's Children's Hospice
- Action on Addition

- Place2Be
- Natural History Museum
- SportsAid
- The 1851 Trust

She is also a joint patron of 100 Women in Hedge Funds' philanthropic initiatives, along with William and Harry.

Kate is a local volunteer leader with the Scout Association in North Wales.

In October 2012, Kate gave her royal backing to the M-PACT program (Moving Parents and Children Together), one of the only UK programs to focus specifically on the impact of drug addiction on families as a whole.

## Honors and Awards

Kate was awarded the Queen Elizabeth II Diamond Jubilee Medal on February 6, 2012.

She currently holds an honorary military appointment in the United Kingdom of honorary air commandant of the Air Training Corps and in Canada of a Canadian Ranger.

## Coat of Arms

Shortly before Kate's wedding, her father was granted a coat of arms. It has three acorns, representing Michael and Carol's three children. Acorns were chosen because oak trees surrounded the area in which the children were raised in West Berkshire. Oak is also a symbol of both England and strength. The gold chevron at the center of the arms represents Carole, whose maiden name is Goldsmith. The thinner white chevrons were designed to reflect the love of the outdoors that the family has, and represent hills and mountains. The red and blue colors reflect the colors on the United Kingdom's flag. All of Michael's children and their descendants have the right to the arms, and as such, Kate's coat of arms was displayed alongside William's on their wedding program, although Kate's arms were suspended from a ribbon to denote that she was unmarried.

In September 2013, a new conjugal coat of arms was released, combining the coat of arms of both William (granted to him by the queen on his 18th birthday) and Kate. A royal lion and unicorn, William's "supporters," surround both shields, each wearing a three-pointed collar. Kate's shield also has a wreath encircling it to balance out the blue garter that encircles William's, resulting from his position as a knight of the Order of the Garter.

# Relationship with William

Kate's relationship with William has been filled with affectionate moments and fun, as opposed to the more formal demeanor between other royal couples such as

Queen Elizabeth II and Prince Philip, Prince Charles and the Princess of Wales, and later, Prince Charles and the Duchess of Cornwall.

Kate and William are often seen sharing small intimate exchanges in public, including during their wedding, and a trip to the Pembroke Refinery in Wales on November 8, 2014.

Plenty of images have captured them sharing a smile or laugh—such as during the World War One 100 Years Commemoration Ceremony in Liege, Belgium, on August 4, 2014; as they received a teddy bear while visiting Macrost Park in Crieff, Scotland, on May 29, 2014; as Kate attempted to spin records while visiting a youth community center in Adelaide, Australia, on April 23, 2014; and as they both tried archery during their tour of Bhutan on April 14, 2016—or making funny faces at each other as they wore 3-D glasses at the Natural History Museum on December 11, 2013; or gazing at each other adoringly, as shown in the glance Kate gave William as they took a tour of the UNICEF warehouse in Denmark on November 2, 2011, or a similar glance Kate gave William as he helped her into her suit during a visit to the Canadian Rangers station in Blatchford Lake, Canada, on July 5, 2011.

One of their most playful moments occurred on April 26, 2013, when they pretended to cast spells on one another at the inauguration of Warner Bros. Studios Leavesden in London. They also display a playful competitiveness, as shown in the image captured of William peeking over Kate's shoulder at her artwork as Kate and William attempted to paint at the Inner City Arts in Los Angeles on July 10, 2011.

William and Kate also share jokes at their own and each other's expense. For example, during a gala on June 23, 2016, Kate joked that the five-course banquet was a welcome reprieve for William, who had to otherwise put up with her cooking. He responded by saying, "It's the reason I'm so skinny." William is not immune to teasing, however; during a visit to the Royal Easter Show at Sydney Olympic Park in Australia on April 18, 2014, they watched an alpaca-shearing demonstration. When the shearer showed them a tuft of alpaca wool of a similar shade to William's hair, Kate suggested that he put it on his head, pointing at his bald spot, to which he laughed.

They are also not shy about physically displaying their affection either, as shown when Kate placed her arm over William's shoulder as they took their dog, Lupo, on a walk on January 12, 2012; or by walking hand in hand, such as on August 1, 2011, when they strolled through Holyrood Park in Edinburgh, Scotland, during their walk to the Christmas Day service at Sandringham estate in 2013, and during their hike in Bhutan; or in sharing a jubilant embrace such as on August 2, 2012, during the London Olympic Games.

While visiting the National September 11 Memorial Museum in New York City on December 9, 2014, William held an umbrella that he shared with Kate. He was again just as attentive as he reached to cover Kate with an umbrella during their visit to Auckland, New Zealand, on April 11, 2014. Kate, likewise, demonstrated her caring and down-to-earth side by holding an umbrella over William as he climbed into a WWI aircraft at the Omaka Aviation Heritage Centre in Blenheim, New Zealand, on April 10, 2014.

It is these beautiful moments between the couple that suggest this fairytale story will be something we will be enjoying for many more years.

# About the Author

Benjamin Southerland is a lifelong Chicagoland resident. Southerland developed a strong interest for politics and government during his college years through his study of leaders who have shaped history, such as Winston Churchill, Napoleon, and Thomas Jefferson. Southerland is also interested in individuals who have impacted the world of sports and entertainment. He has studied and written about politicians, world leaders, athletes, and celebrities. He researches these fascinating figures extensively in order to determine what has shaped their worldviews and contributed to their success. He aims for his books to give readers a deep understanding of the achievements, inspirations, and goals of the world's most influential individuals. Follow Benjamin Southerland at his website benjaminsoutherland.com to learn about his latest books.

Printed in Great Britain
by Amazon